AMIDST TIME THAT WAITS

AMIDST TIME THAT WAITS

Selected Poetry and Spoken Word

PJ

PHOENIX JAMES

AMIDST TIME THAT WAITS

Copyright © 2025 Prince-James Harrison.

All rights reserved.

No part of this publication may be reproduced, distributed, or transmitted in any form or by any means, including photocopying, recording, or other electronic or mechanical methods, without the prior written permission of the publisher, except in the case of brief quotations embodied in critical reviews and certain other noncommercial uses permitted by copyright law.

For any questions about usage, please email contact@PhoenixJamesOfficial.com

First Edition: 2025

ISBN: 978-1-0685383-6-0 (Paperback)

Cover Artwork & Design by Phoenix James.
Book Design & Formatting by Phoenix James.

Visit the author's website at www.PhoenixJamesOfficial.com or email him at phoenix@PhoenixJamesOfficial.com

Time holds its breath,
and walks alongside you.

CONTENTS

ALL USED UP 1
ALMOST DROWNED 4
CLOSER 6
DREAMS 7
FOR ALL TIME 8
FUTURE WE 9
GLORY DAY 17
HIGH OFF THIS MOMENT 21
I HAVEN'T THOUGHT ABOUT SEX IN A WHILE 24
I LIKE PROGRESS MORE THAN SLEEP 26
IN KNOWING YOURSELF 29
IN THE GOING DOWN 31
INEVITABLY CHANGE COMES 32
KNOW WHEN IT'S TIME 35
LANGUAGE OF THE FUTURE 36
MAYBE TODAY 40
MOMENTS IN TIME 49
NO RETREAT, NO SURRENDER 51
OF A BROKEN WORLD 55
ONE STONE A DAY 57
PATIENCE OVERALL 60
PRESERVATION OF THE PRICELESS 65
REMEMBER YOU, REMEMBER ME 72
SAD IN A LITTLE WAY 77
SELF REFLECTIONS 78
THE ENDING OF HUMANITY 85
THE GAME OF LIFE II 90
THE ONLY THING FOREVER IS CHANGE 94
THE TIME I STOOD HER UP 102
THE ULTIMATE GOAL 105
THIS IS NOT THE END 108
TO BE SOMEWHERE ELSE 111
TOMORROW 114
TOUCH THE SUN 118
TRANSCRIBING THE FUTURE 121
UNTIL THEN 124
WHEN I'M GONE 125
WONDER OF THE SOUL 129
YOUR AUTHOR 130

ALL USED UP

I hope you
Save or hold nothing back
Of yourself in this life
I hope you learn to let go
Let go until your heart
And your palms are light
And bare
Until you free your feet
And give birth to wings
Until your mind and spirit
Find peace
I hope you lay it all out
All of it
Everything
Everything you came with
Everything you now have
All you collected
And accumulated
Learned and gathered
And became attached
To carrying with you
Along your way
Those treasures
You forgot you had

Buried somewhere inside
I hope you discover them again
One day
When something feels absent
And you're not sure where you are
I hope you leave them all here
Your light and your dark places
All that you are
All that you were
And have to give now
Leave them behind
For others to find
Here where our gifts
Are only given to us
To be given away
Just like your brilliant smile
It is of no worth to you
Until it is presented
To another
Here
Where you are of most use
As was intended
Here
Where light begets light
And chases away shadows
By the time your wings

Take you beyond this place
I hope you have left
Nothing of your self
I hope you take nothing
Of your value with you
That you leave
Each and every one
Of your special little
Precious gems behind
That your soul floats lightly
In the knowing
That you gave
Much more than you took
I hope you rise
Filled abundantly
With all life gave you
But yet satisfyingly empty
Not a thing unseen
Unshared
Unsaid
Undiscovered
Or undone
When you leave
May it be with an empty cup
By such time
I hope you're all used up.

ALMOST DROWNED

I went on a school trip
To Wales
When I was about ten
I got into the swimming pool
I ended up in the deep end
I couldn't swim
I started drowning
I went down twice
I went down the third time
They say you go up
And down
Three times
Before you drown
The last time I went down
A man pulled me up
At that moment
I was scratching at his legs
Drowning basically
I guess he realised
At that point
That I might be drowning
It was a while though
Before he actually reacted
And pulled me out

I feel if not for that
I might not be here
Right now
I always remember that
I think I've always
Had a little fear
Of the water
Since that time
I was ten years old
I never forget that
Wales school trip
Nearly died at ten
I'm glad I didn't
Nearly was a goner
I stopped
Going in the water
As much
I definitely had a fear of it
I've been
In a lot deeper water since
Both literally
And figuratively.

CLOSER

I care not
That the earth
Is becoming smaller
That the seas
Are rising
To drown
And consume the planet
That global warming
Is melting the ice caps
That the oceans
Are corroding the coastlines
I threw away
My old atlas
I don't care how much
The new one has changed
The smaller
Our vulnerable
Little island becomes
The better it is
For I pray
That it will close our distance
And drift you
Closer to me
One day.

DREAMS

Long before
I'd ever heard the words
Time makes dreams defer
I had defaced every clock face
And replaced them
With images of her
So now I only picture
The face
Of a missed universe
She gives my dreams
Their place
And worth
While mother nature
Remains
Lost for words
Clutching
At the fading skirt
Of mother earth
I'm disco dancing
With eternity
She vows to serve me
Time fades
It's cursed
I dream
Eternally.

FOR ALL TIME

I love the iconic figures
I watched as a kid
Like Audrey Hepburn
And Marilyn Monroe
And so on
We'll all be forgotten
Eventually
In the sands of time
Even the most famous
And influential of us
Or maybe not
Maybe since their era
And others like them
We've found a way
To preserve ourselves
For all time
Maybe
Maybe not
Perhaps the earth
Will take it all back one day
To dust
Everything
But since you're reading this
I guess they survived.

FUTURE WE

I often think
About contacting you
Yet I am still afraid
I shall explain
I'd be taking a huge step forward
After years and years of relationships
With women
Much
And I mean much too much
The wrong choice for myself
And I, I would say, wrong for them too
But that's not the problem
I have endured a lot
In those long years
Giving chances
Wanting it to work
But here I have given up
I am at peace on my own
But the leap of faith
I have been taking
Dating again
Is still early
As I have to put my thoughts right
In other words

What I've been thinking is
I would like a serious relationship
Which would build up slowly
But surely
And to reach this
Both the man and the woman
Have to ensure
That the boxes
Are ticked in, to achieve this
I have often worried I'm getting old
Only to realise
It's becoming the opposite
Which fills me
With much optimism
I have been with good intentions
And successful in them thus far
To change my diet
My old habits
To return to the gym
I am pleased with progress
Those around me notice
And commend and applaud this
Tell me I do not need it
But my mirror told me I did
I wouldn't consider me a 'party boy'
But I can entertain a whole room

With my charisma
I love music
Dancing
I'm not a professional
But I have all the rhythm
Wish I did more with it
The second important thing for me
Or I should have put it at number one
Is my religion
I am an artist
Another devout rebel of the world
Genius level creativity
And prolific
There's much to show and share
And I guess equally plenty to tell
Perhaps for when we meet
But that creative nature
Is rooted in my DNA
I know you'll understand it
That and my God are one
My mind is more open now than ever
From experience
I have learnt that it is important
That both people in a relationship
Have the same faith
Or can relate to one another's

It's not as common
In relationships
As one would expect
Hope
Or desire
As being yoked to unbelievers
Is a disobedience to one's self
And a necessity to be yoked
If both share the same faith
I don't know what your age will be
If you'll be younger
Or older than me
Not that it matters too much
Right now at least
I have vowed
That I will never
Make the same mistakes again
Though since then
I've made the error of repeating them
I'm making them much less now
As I did as a younger man
Will you want to start a family
If we do so decide
By such time
I hope it's a thing
We can both supply

I feel otherwise
It might make one
Or both of us
Feel inadequate
Useless perhaps
And preventing the other party
From having their desire for such
The hurt might be too much
The straw that breaks the camel's back
Will you want promise of marriage
Who knows
We haven't even met
Once in a while
My faith in such regards
For a brief time, is renewed
By someone I've been close to
But mostly by the thought of you
I've been torn
I've been burned
I've been broken
For the simple reason
I only wanted to be married once
I was always the boy of the fairytale
When you become him
He's hard to leave behind
Which of the two of us will die first

Leaving the other behind
To the emptiness of what was
To the loneliness
Of what can no longer be
Will we want to marry again
And have still a family
Why not
There's nothing wrong with that
I'd encourage it to be
If it is you I should leave
Here to exist without me
Perhaps rather a conversation
For after we at least meet
Please do excuse me
Seated in all that's been wrong
Reasons
For never ever
Wanting to be married
And all the lies
And the broken promises
The lies and the deceit
And the pain
That hurt so much
That it is beyond words
I am now healing
Trying not to look back

Yet not wanting to misstep
By having chosen to forget
Hence, corresponding here
To start to reach you
Is what I would be happy to do
To start that journey
I am open and transparent
As there's no point in pretending
Or glossing over the truth
For in the long run
What good does it do
So, I hope you'll feel comfortable
With what I am saying to you
Wait, what am I saying
It's you
I know you will
I know you do
I know you know
That there are children to be freed
And we are all and each free agents
Grown but still in need
And no need so much to be polite
I believe that everybody here
In this place
Is looking for something serious
Or at least something meaningful

Which is not built overnight
Hence it is best, in this case
Not to hide anything from you
Nor you from me
When we do eventually meet
Rather than expose our truth later
And end up both displeased
Wanting to break free.

GLORY DAY

Their spirit
Constantly serves to remind me
She is coming
So I keep myself here
Always in preparation
For her arrival
These ancient men say
She passes your way
Only but once
So I continue pressing on
I wish to be ready
When she comes
And when she does
I will not be afraid
I will go
Peacefully along her way
I pray
She will accept my humble efforts
And see them as worthy
Of her presence
I yearn for her acceptance
This I long for everyday
And a shooting star
Still confirms my birthright

Over a million miles away
And I am here
With the love of angels
Within my circumference
So why should I fear
Here where the rhythm of silence
Now is as beautiful
As when I speak
These wonders
I have been told in whispers
In stares
And gestures
Breaths of hope
Here where my full moon
Is so much fuller now
Means so much more now
Again
The sky never lapses
Still paints pictures that say
This is what men of honour quest for
These are what the stones
Of the builder look like
This is the colour
Of the bricks on the road
This way leads to your fortress
And this is where the fork is

Beware
Time is friend or foe
Always
Though you decide
Which way the spoon bends
And when
Outside of your hands
Is how soon it ends
Always
And I adore the message
This landscape conveys
It shines more beautiful
And says more
Than I could ever hope to portray
And that's okay
I know my place
And that she is coming for me
Like the men of old say
I know her face
I see her in my dreams everyday
I will welcome her
With all and everything inside me
That desires her more
Than any living thing
She's worth dying for
My beautiful children

Will know me best
Through her
And because my overbearing
Determination
Has and will always
Continue to drive me
In pursuit of her
They will be blessed
And highly favoured
And remembered
In life
And even in death
As will their father
And their children
I will carry this
And bear it forever
Until she comes for me
And I will go peacefully
And freely
As if it were merely death
Softly calling me
Rather than glory
My day cometh
And I live for it
This is my story.

HIGH OFF THIS MOMENT

How amazing it would be
If you could go into a place
Or a platform like YouTube now
And you could look up
Your great-great granddad
Or great-great-great-great granddddad
Or grandmother
Doing something
Like boiling an egg
Or talking to a friend
About a new pair of shoes they bought
And how they either like them
Or don't like them
Or for what reason they like them
Just having a random conversation
Nothing that would be anything
To anyone else but you
How amazing that would be
How much do you think
That privilege would be worth
If you could go and do that
Just go on the internet
And just see way back
To where you came from

Way down the line
Your great-great-great grandmother
Or great-great-great-great granddad
Just tying his shoelace or something
If we had shoelaces back then
I think that would be so amazing
The thing is
You now are that
That great-great-great-great
Great grandparent
Whether you're a sister
Whether you are a daughter
Whether you are an auntie
You are that person now
You're that person
That someone in the future
Generations and generations
In the future
Will be looking back to see
Seeing where they came from
You're that person now in history
And time
Within this very moment
You're that person
That someone is going to be
Looking back for

Looking at your nose
Looking at your lips
Listening to your voice
Looking at what you wore
Thinking how much they look like you
Or the mannerisms that they have
They can actually see they came from you
How amazing is that
To say, Oh look
That's where my eyebrows came from
It's crazy when you think about it
We're living in that time now
Where people are going to be able
To reference back
And see that stuff
Because the technology is here now
It's here
We're living it
It's amazing
I'm high off of this moment
That we're living in right now.

I HAVEN'T THOUGHT ABOUT SEX IN A WHILE

I haven't thought about sex in a while
Wild I know
But true
To tell the truth
I haven't even thought about you
It would be a lie
If I said I thought about your smile
Or the things we used to do
At least not in the way
You'd love me to
I always seem to end up
Right back here in this stuff
Feeling like I didn't make it clear enough
That I'm never really making love
As much as I'm sincerely fucking up
The smart ones run a mile
The smarter ones
Two or three
Once they come to decide
That just one of them
Is no match for two of me
Me and all of my seasons
Your reasons for not believing

You and all of your demons
Fighting to shadow box with mine
You naked wearing all of my semen
And me in nothing more than a good time
But I haven't thought about sex in a while
And the thought of that makes me smile.

I LIKE PROGRESS MORE THAN SLEEP

Good morning
Been up since 4 a.m
It's 5 a.m now
So I've been up an hour
Gathering my thoughts
It's a good time to be awake
When the earth is still relatively still
And one can think
Before the busy world awakes
And everything is moving
And motion
I like to exist in the stillness
I like to be awake in it
And have that space
To let my thoughts travel
Travel beyond the busy city
Or before the busy city
When the earth is still relatively quiet
Uninterrupted thoughts can travel
Just thinking time basically
I like it
It's all very quiet
Even at this time
Even the 5 a.m

It's just relatively still
At least where I am
Due to get up shortly
And start my day
This is actually a lie-in for me
That's funny
A lot of the time I'm up at 3 a.m
To seize the day
It's interesting what motivates you
To get up
Or wake up
And be productive
When there's no one telling you to
When there's no one forcing you to
When there's no boss
Breathing down your neck
To arrive at his workplace for this time
Or that time
It definitely feels
Like you're doing something pretty amazing
When you can do that yourself
When you don't have to
It definitely adds to your day
Those extra hours that you sacrifice
By getting up early
Before the rest of the world

Makes such a difference
When by 10 a.m
You've already pretty much
Completed your day
And the rest of the day is yours
To do whatever you want to do
That's a nice place to be at
So I enjoy waking up at 3 a.m
Even when people would say
You don't have to
I like it
Because I just like progress
More than I like sleep
And so I will sacrifice sleeping in
When I don't have to
I don't have to sleep in
It's a choice
I can wake up
And do what I have to do
And it feels good
It feels majorly good
I'm off to start my day
Enjoy yours.

IN KNOWING YOURSELF

Finding yourself
Is a never-ending
Ongoing journey
Our self discovery
Is forever in motion
The world we exist in
Is ever-changing
The energy
Of the consistently
Expanding universe
We draw ourselves from
Is never still
The planet
And everything on
Around
And within it
Is constantly shifting
Knowledge of self therefore
Is not a point to be reached
It is an arrival
At one destination
From another
While on route to the next
There's always more to teach

There's always more to learn
There's always room to grow
And there's forever more to know
Nothing alive stays the same
We are never in the same space
Same way
Same place
Evolve
Evolve more
Then evolve again
Repeat.

IN THE GOING DOWN

Life is so brief
That we only realise it
At the end
And it's sad
It's sad that
We don't see
The things
That really matter
Until it's towards
The end of that life.

INEVITABLY CHANGE COMES

After ten years
Even seven years
You're going to
Watch that person change
As you're changing
At one point
When you get married
You may even
Be at the same place
But then
Depending on
Who you are as people
You're both going to evolve
And change
And it's interesting
Seeing that change
And where it might veer off
Where you each veer off
Away from each other
As opposed to getting closer
Because they're growing
You're growing
Your brains are growing
Your experience of life

Is growing
What you want
Can change as well
As you get older
In your outlook
In your mind
And that can be affected
By things that happened
Years before you met
That forming
Of who you become
And where
You decide you want to go
And decide
That this isn't
What you want anymore
And drift away
That could have been
Something that was there
Before you even got married
Things are instilled
And your wants
And your needs
And your desires
Having children as well
That can alter

Your outlook on life
And change you
That's an important aspect
When the children grow up
And they're not dependent
On both of you anymore
Then they begin leaving
And you both
Have to come back
To yourselves
And then you start to see
The cracks
And the things
That don't align anymore
Or the cracks
Can be already there
But you're so busy
With the children
And everyday life
That you haven't had time
To focus on them
Until the children are gone
Then the cracks
Become more evident
And then it all begins
To fall in on itself.

KNOW WHEN IT'S TIME

It's all about positivity
You just have to know
When it's necessary
To separate yourself
From certain things
And certain people
Because you just know
No good
Is going to come of it
So you've just
Got to know
When that time is
And be perceptive
Tune into your
Perceptive energy
And just know
When it's time
To separate yourself
From certain people
And certain things
No going back.

LANGUAGE OF THE FUTURE

I think
Going back to
The subject
Of our youngsters
Being at a disadvantage
If we don't allow them
To have the freedom
To explore where the world is going
Like the basics
Imagine
You have children now
Who, aside from school
When they have to put pen to paper
Which again, is questionable
A lot of stuff is done on computers now
But like simply writing things down
On a piece of paper
If they're not texting
Or doing it on an iPad
Or a computer screen
They're not used to that
They're not in that habit
Of getting the pen
And paper

And a pencil even
And writing something down
A note, a number, an address
They're just not in that routine
So imagine
When they have to now go
And be without their phone
Or that type of technology
That they're used to so much
They're going to be kind of stuck
Like, how do I write again
How do I spell
Because on a mobile phone
They know exactly where every key is
With their eyes closed
But give them the alphabet
And a pen and paper
And write some words down
They may be a little stuck
I get it saves time
To write the number '2'
Instead of the word 'too'
But it's one of my peeves
In one sense
We've got to kind of respect it
Because they've created a text language

There is a language
That has been created now
Which is your shorthand today
From yesterday's shorthand
Klingon on is a language
Who knows
The way the youngsters are writing now
And a lot of adults too
The way they shorten words
And write numbers
Instead of the actual word
Or they write the letter 'c' instead of 'see'
What will happen in the future
Will people not understand
What the hell that says
Or what that means
Or will it be like
The new form of hieroglyphics
For the future
Will people look at it on walls
Or on computers
And understand it
Like this is the ancient language
Or would they be like
What the hell is this
We don't understand this one

We understand this, this is English
We remember this
This is what our ancestors used
Our ancestors spoke English
We understand this
They called this English in their time
We understand this
But what is this other thing here
What is this other language
We don't understand this..
C u l8r
Or is it going to be a derivative
Are they going to look at it as
A derivative from English
It's interesting
We will see, I guess
Time will tell, I should say
Rather than, we will see
Because you and I won't be around.

MAYBE TODAY

Sometimes
We fail to see the light
Maybe today
It'll shine bright
And maybe today
We'll find
Some peace of mind
Because only God knows
How long we've been trying
To see some sun shine
Through
On the things we do
And who's to say
Today
We may see a way through
The troubles and strife
And even though everyday life
Throws another roll of the dice
We learn to play our hand
Even when our cards ain't nice

And we don't quit
Even when our hardest hit
We stick to it

Because you can never tell
How close you are
It may be near
When it seems so far
Remember
Everyone's a shining star
With a capable chemistry to achieve
Anything they want to
If they believe
And I know it's real
So I take it from here
Where I can feel
An energy
Propelling me
Telling me
To put it down for you
And I will too
Because all the things that affect me
Indirectly affect you

It's true
And it's enough to drive you
Round the bend
When you discover
Another ain't really your friend
But still

Let's get up and try again
My friends
We can't let the negatives
Hold us down
No way
Let's pick our dreams up
From off the ground
And be not so easily swayed
By the troubles
And the turmoils of the day
That seem to float through the air
Instead let's ask ourselves the question
Why are we here?
And even though an equal amount
Simply just don't care
Let's be the ones to make a change
And turn things around this year
And next year
Without fear
Knowing where we're going
Let's keep this karma flowing

It's mind blowing
To know that where the mind goes
The body follows
For the mind controls the body

And thoughts control actions
Now
This is only just a fraction
Of my reaction
To a mother earth
In serious contraction
For all I see
Is grief on the streets
In a city where hearts bear no pity
It's far from pretty
And there sure ain't no unity
In my community
I've been seeing this since puberty
And it's a real calamity
It seems as though
We've forsaken all humanity
I see so many lose their sanity
Over vanity
So I pray for our rationality

As I sow these seeds
And plead
That they won't fall by the wayside
Because of pride
I look at men's lives
And feel uninspired

Because all I see
Is pain inside
And fear in their eyes
I think it's about time we rise
And be extra careful
Not to get roped in
Because it's so easy
To adopt the wrong thing
That's why I sing a song
And try to build a strong team
With a positive theme
So a positive future
Can be seen
Here's hoping
We all achieve our dreams
And my spirit is unrelenting
This is a manifestation
Of the faith that I was sent in
Which liberates me
From my fears
So let all those that have ears
Hear

Because I see a future
Beyond the darkness
I never used to

Because it was never like this
It was dull but it's brighter now
I see blue skies
Beyond the rain filled clouds
And yesterday
Did really end last night
Today's a new day
And it looks bright
I think what I'll do
Is take a vacation
And from now on
Look for the benefits
In every situation
No longer being impatient
Just being the best that I can be

And if you see me on the street
Or at the club
Greet me with enthusiasm
And love
Because
Even though
My mentality
Rises up out of the ghetto
I'm still attached to the stem
Just like a rose petal

Hoping one day
I'll be able to pass by the corners
And not see
The brothers hanging out
Doing the same old things
Smoking
And calling at the women
Every time they came about
But simply had a change of heart
And decided to make a new start

You say
But it's hard in this life
And that
I don't deny
But that doesn't grant you the excuse
Not to try
I mean
Tell me why
Do some stall
While others just fly by
Some take a nose dive
Some fly low
And some fly high
Some are even petrified
So bless those who try

And those who take the time out
To work this rhyme out
Just to find out
What it's all about
Because
Every line counts
That's why I wrote it down

And in the hope
That we should not be like
Lambs to the slaughter
I've led many horses to water
But never been able
To make them drink
Hopefully this one
Will make them think
And begin to look inside themselves
And realise
That there's nothing missing
And that goes for you too
So listen
For as long as the stars glisten
Stay on your mission
And let no soul deter you
From your ambition
It's your decision

To be or not to be
Don't let Mr and Mrs know it all
Control your destiny
And who am I
Phenzwaan
Giving you
The best
In me.

MOMENTS IN TIME

I know there are moments
In time
I know there are moments in time
That are happening
That may never repeat themselves
They may come in other forms
In other ways
But they're not going to come back
In the way they came at that moment
And in that energy that it was in
Or recorded in
The energy that may help somebody
Or I may need to know at that time
Or may need to refer to
In some way down the line
Or that just may be the moment
Sometimes you capture something
And it's that moment
You couldn't have got it a second time
If you try to do it a second time
It's not going to be the same
It's that moment
And thank God
I put on the camera sometimes
And record
Because I would miss so much magic
So much magic
It's going to change

Energy is always evolving
It's always changing
It's always going away
And coming back around
Like how the earth spins
It's going around
It comes back around again
And it meets the sun
And if you miss that
You've got to wait
Another hour
Another day
Another year
You've got to wait
Another hundred years
A thousand million years
For it to come back around again
It's like that
It's a moment
It'll come again
But it won't be the same
And it'll be another time
It won't be that time
And we're not around long enough
To miss those moments
That's how I feel.

NO RETREAT, NO SURRENDER

Why just recite poetry
When I can turn words
To sodium nitrate
Ignite each verse
Watch it explode
And feel my soul vibrate
Shaking demons off
Propelling me closer
To my dreams and goals
And the achievement of
It's expensive
Keeping the flame alight though
You wouldn't believe the cost
Sacrifice
Sometimes
You have to die to be alive
So I don't grieve the loss
And as long as
I can still taste
The sulphur on my lips
I know I can burn every vulture
Off that cliff
And what can you tell me
Nothing

Until you know what it is
To be down in that valley
Surrounded
Praying
That the fables aren't true
But praying to who
They say god left this place
Long before you were born
So that leaves them
And you
In a dusty torn robe
Grazed elbows
And dirty finger nails
From scratching at the stones
Trying to escape
To some other place
Doesn't matter
Just somewhere else
We create our world
And try to escape from our self
Tripping over
At every attempt
As though our feet were tied
Falling to our knees
Crying to the skies
Begging for time

To slow down
So we can
Catch a piece of the sun
Before it disappears
Behind the horizon
And now
That your time has come
Have no regrets
Except
That you couldn't
Tell somebody sooner
That when the solar rays
That radiate their day
Fade away
That they could use the moonlight
To illuminate their night
Just as bright
That no condition
Is permanent
And that it's okay to cry
That even the wise
Are still learning
And that in every wrong
There's a right
I don't care
If you have to lay booby traps

And tripwire
Through the forest
Plant letter bombs
In their mailboxes
Wire live grenades
To their doorframes
Detonate dynamite
Under their cars
Desecrate their places of worship
Set fire to their gods
Use violence
Use politics
Use sex
Use science
Peace keep with guns
Drop bombs
And demand silence
Get them
Demand their attention
And when they're listening
Tell them
The only thing consistent
Is change
And therefore
Things are only permanent
Temporarily.

OF A BROKEN WORLD

I think we're all broken
Before we get here
We are born
Of broken people
Who too
Were born of broken people
As were those before them
We are all products
Of a broken world
A breaking planet
With a nature
To give birth to things
Only to watch them die
Like a wilting flower
A dying fruit
A fallen tree
A decaying building
An eroding coastline
A fading sunset
We are no exception
There is nothing held onto
That subconscious
Realisation
In itself

Breaks you
Those who live
Under the illusion
That we aren't inherently
Born broken
Break the most
Life is a journey
Spent finding
Putting
Or keeping
All of our little
Broken pieces
Of ourselves
Together
For as long as we can.

ONE STONE A DAY

I've already impressed myself
Looking back
At what I've achieved
In the past year
Looking back at things I did
A year ago
And feeling impressed with myself
Proud of myself
Looking back a year ago to today
Things I did then
And from then till this point now
I'm feeling
That sense of accomplishment
And a sense of achievement
I'm actually doing it
It's nice
And that's just twelve months
So I imagine
How I would feel
In twenty-four months
Forty-eight months and so on
My friend always says
A stone a day raises a tower
And it's so true

A stone a day
And before you know it
You've got that sky high tower
That you've built yourself
Do I have off days
Feeling down
I don't have off days
If anything
I have off moments
And it's not long
Before I'm back in the right mode
In the positive mode
Back in the opposite to off day
I'm back on to on day very quickly
Just because of my wiring
And my conditioning
And things
That I've conditioned my mind with
That help me get back
Just understanding state changes
All the stuff I've learned from NLP
All of that just helps me
To not stay in that place
For very long at all
So I'll have off moments
But I'll never have off days

No way
I'll have off moments
Where I'll contemplate something
Or think negatively about something
Or feel off about something
Or down
But it won't really last long at all
I'm back in the swing in no time
It happens because I'm human
We're human
And it's likely to happen
I'm not He-Man
As much as I would like to be
Or as much as I think I am
I'm not
I'll be back in no time
One stone a day
Raises a tower.

PATIENCE OVERALL

The big one I learned
Is the one
That I will share
It's patience
Patience
Is so important
First and foremost
Top of the list
Patience
Lack of
Can ruin a lot
Of opportunities
Can stop a lot
Of progress
Can hinder you
Other side notes
To that
Don't be afraid
To do things
On your own
Don't think
That you're only
One person
That you're limited

And cannot
Make things happen
A lot of individual people
On their own
Have made a lot
Of things
Happen
If we look at history
A lot of single people
Without a team
Have made things happen
Then teams
Wanted to get involved
When they saw
That this
One person
Was able to
Do this thing
Not everybody had a team
To start with
So don't be afraid
To do things
On your own
Is another side thing
To that
But overall

Patience
Patience
Patience
Patience
Sometimes
We are like me
As I was
I should say
Early in the process
Wasn't patient
At the time
I had a vision
That no one else
Really saw
At the time
Or very few
People saw
Or at least
The circles I was in
Didn't see
And because of that
I started to question
My vision
And all it was
Is that
I was early

In the process
And didn't
Have the patience
To see it through
And just keep going
And it hindered me
And it's only after
Experiencing that
That I learned
What had happened
And having to reset
So my advice
Would be
Patience
Overall
Patience
Is so important
And it can
Add a lot to you
When you're patient
You think it's
Taking away
We often think
Patience
Is taking away
From us

Waiting
But often
It's adding
And that's something
I wish
I knew
As a youngster.

PRESERVATION OF THE PRICELESS

Writing
Making films
Video blogging
Just ideas
And things
That I've thought about
That I've not really
Heard anyone else
Speak about
Or crazy ideas
That are true to life
But don't
Necessarily exist
That I'd like to
Explore
And open up
People's minds to
I like a lot of the things
I create
I take pleasure
In knowing
That it's going to
Stimulate conversation
Or in the very least

If not external
Open conversation
With other people
That it's going to create
Internal dialogue
For people
They'll see or hear it
And they'll go away
And think about things
In a different way
From the way
They were thinking about them
And I love that whole thing
And also
It kind of
Gives a little opening
To my mind as well
How I think
And my thoughts
And little
Pieces of myself
Are being shared
I got very strongly
Into vlogging
A lot because
I realise

There's two things
That are happening
It's something
I did before
But I kind of left off
Like ten years ago
And I kind of got back into it
Got passionate about it again
There's two things
That are happening
In creating videos and stuff
I get to satisfy
My creative need
Desire
Lust
Whatever you
Want to call it
And I also look at
How much I would
Love to go back now
And be able to
Go online for example
And pull up a video of my
Great-great great-great-great
Grandparents
And watch them

Doing something
No matter how random
Watch them sitting
At a table eating food
Or watch them
Getting ready
On their way to work
Watch them
With their children
Or parents
Taking them to school even
Or just sitting talking
About how
Disgusting this drink is
Or whatever
Just the joy that would be
How precious
And priceless
That would be
For me to be able
To go online and do that
Of course I can't
Because that material
Doesn't exist
The second thing is
As I was saying

About what's satisfying
And gratifying for me
Is the fact that
I know I'm creating
That same thing
For my descendants
So they will have something
To pull up
And look at
And reference
Where they came from
Their lineage
Their ancestors
Their great-great-great-great
Grandparents
Or granddad
It's like preservation
For those
Who will come after
And satisfying my own
Creative desires
In the present
And sharing
I learn a lot
About myself
When I make a vlog

Or video
Or whatever
I learn a lot about myself
Sometimes I just
Put the camera on
And just let it go
And just speak
Because I never know
What I'm going to
Speak about that day
Sometimes I have a topic
In mind
Sometimes I don't
I'll just speak
And I learn a lot
About myself
And I know in turn
Other people
Will learn something
And on it goes
There's a lot of things
Happening
One of the things
I've learned
Is that I can just
Do what I just said

Putting the camera on
And just going
Just talking
And seeing what comes
And things that are
In my mind
I didn't know
Were there
Or you forgot
That you'd learned
Or experienced
Or encountered
What I've really learned
Is that nothing
Is lost
Nothing is gone
Any experience
That you have
You think it's
A far distant thing
And that's definitely
One of the things
I've learned
That nothing is lost
Everything is there.

REMEMBER YOU, REMEMBER ME

Remember you
Remember me
We used to share the same energy
Vibrate off of the same frequencies
Our self conduct was nothing but decency
We used to be care free from material wear
We were so in tune with our humanity
Didn't know vanity
We moved more mentally
Than mechanically
Remember you
Remember me
How we used to walk
Across the blue sea effortlessly
How you would talk to me
And I would talk to you
Through telepathy
We were so free
Didn't need weed
Or Hennessy
To get high
Or to get by
We were so in sync
With our own minds

That we could even fly
Remember those times
Picked our own grapes
From our own vines
And boy
Did we make some fine wines
And do I need remind you
Of when we sat around the fire
And intertwined rhymes too
Until it was time to retire
How we clapped our hands
And clicked our fingers
And stamped our feet
To the same drumbeat
How you would run
And I would count
And you would hide
And I would seek
That was our game
Nothing really changed
Except now
They play it in the physical
We used to play it in the brain
Remember
How we used to read the stars
And the constellations

And how we didn't have to visit bars
To get good conversation
Or smoke their cigarettes
How dare we forget
Shame on you
Shame on me
Look at us
With their stuff
We're even wearing their clothes
Don't you know
We wore the finest robes
Whilst sat on the highest thrones
Didn't worship material things though
No mobile phones
On our long distance trips
But still we were equipped
To phone home
Remember me
Remember you
Growing our own food
So plentiful
Going to the same school
Our parents were the teachers
We lived by the same rules
No religious preachers

To keep us fooled
So high in our spirituality
We had one to ones too
With our creators
And that was cool
Remember those times
When fruit and water
Was just enough
Used to live in our heads then
Not in our guts
Yeah
That was us
Vibing off of each others intellect
See
No BBC
No Sky Digital
No TV
So how could you neglect me
Or me neglect you
I was your entertainment
You were mine
I had to respect you
Trying to get through
Trying to get you to see
The bigger picture
How it was

Now we're out
In the wilderness
Can't remember
Where we lived
We must be lost
It's true
We must because
You can't remember me
And I can only just
Remember you.

SAD IN A LITTLE WAY

It's sad to think
That we're only
A blip in time
Like a raindrop in the ocean
In regards to how long
We'll exist time
Time is a vast ocean
And we're only a raindrop in it
We won't get to see
All the world
All the beauties
Of the whole planet
We won't get to see half of it
There's so much to see
So much to experience
And we couldn't possibly
See all of it
So we'll miss so much
During our very brief stay
Our trip almost seems wasted
For how much we won't see
We arrive and depart in a day
Life doesn't let you see it all
It's kind of sad in a little way.

SELF REFLECTIONS

A lot of the time
People don't like what they see
They don't like that reflection
They don't like
What you represent for them
Nothing wrong with you
What offends them
Is the fact that who you are
Shows them who they're not
Who they feel they should be
But they're not
It's an interesting one
Reflection
Mirror
Representation
It's you shining your light
Without even knowing
On them
And them being able
To see themselves
Seeing what they want
What they're not
What they want to be
What they wish they could be

They don't hate you
They don't dislike you
And if they do
If we can say that
It's not because of anything
You've done that is wrong
It's to do with
What you show them to be
To themselves
Like a mirror
Like a reflection
They see you
They see themselves
They're either like you
Or they're not
And they either like that fact
Or they don't
So don't worry about you
You're fine
You're doing just fine
Do you
Keep doing you
As you've been doing you
And don't worry about haters
Don't worry about dislikers
Don't worry about people

Dissing your ambitions
And trying to put you down
And belittle you
And all of that stuff
You know it
Because you've experienced it
You may be experiencing it
Right now
But I tell you
From my experience
It's not that they
Don't like you
It's nothing you're doing wrong
You keep doing what you're doing
It's something
That they have to deal with
You're a representation
Of what they wish they could be
Perhaps you show them
What they're not
And they don't have
An easy time with it
So every time
You come around
You're an offence to them
You're offensive

And it's a lot to do with that
Don't take that to heart at all
Just keep doing you
Hopefully they'll come around
And realise that they can do
Just as you're doing
Be just as you are
Or better
For themselves
It's not you
It's nothing to do with you
It's nothing you need to change
Or any way you need to be
Don't take it on board
You can't
You just can't afford to
People need to
Deal with themselves
Basically
Keep shining your light
And being who you are
Just do that
Just keep being who you are
It's not about you
It's not that they don't like you
It's not you at all

It's them
If they were in a different place
Within themselves
They would love you
So it's not about you
Just as you are
They would love you
It's not about you
They dislike the reflection
That you cast
And it's not your fault
You're just being yourself
You show them
Where they're lacking
Where they're not whole
You show them
The inadequacies
Within themselves
Just by being you
And shining your light
And being a reflection
Of the world
It's not about you
It's none of your business
What people
Who are not happy

With themselves
Are doing
Or saying
Negatively against you
It is of no benefit to you
It's none of your business
It is of no value to you
It doesn't progress you
In any way
So don't focus on it
Just keep doing you
It's nothing
That you need to
Worry about
That you need to change
It's something
That they need to deal with
And hopefully
They will in time
So that they can progress
So that they can advance
To where they're in a place
That doesn't
Make them feel a way
Whenever they see you
When they see you

Progressing
None of your business
None of your regard
Nothing for you to
Worry about
Just keep doing you
Keep shining
And keep growing
Keep moving forward
Keep putting one foot
In front of the other
In the right direction
And when you see
You're making progress
And people
Are not liking it
Keep going.

THE ENDING OF HUMANITY

I believe the world is on a decline
I believe it's ending bit by bit
Not the globe is going to blow up
Or the planet earth is going to blow up
But ending in terms of humanity
I feel our human-ness
And our humane humanity is declining
I feel like humanity is reduced a lot
And it's declining
More and more as time goes on
I really believe
Things like smartphones and technology
And this desire to have things now
And time being sped up
All these things that we accumulate
And design and use
To save time
And get things quicker
I feel that has taken some of the humanity
Away from us
We're losing patience
And that's part of our humanity
To be patient
We're losing that

Because everyone wants everything now
And fast
And computers
And now now now now now
We're just losing the ability
To sit down and have a conversation
Without being distracted
I feel that's how the world is ending
The world as in human
The human nature is ending
As we slowly go towards
Becoming androids and robots
The robots are taking over
And eventually
They'll kill all the humanity in us
Completely
Until we're just walking robots
And androids ourselves
Who used to be human
Or at least we still appear human
But we're not
There's no human element left
Because everything is operated digitally
And everything's at the touch of a button
The flick of a switch
Or they're activated by voice

No one will have time
For sitting down
And having conversations anymore
It's all about information now
How quick can I get the information
How quickly can I transfer the information
The human element was
When you asked somebody
How they're doing
You listened back to the response
There wasn't all of this distraction
In the middle
Where you don't even listen
To if they've actually answered the question
The person has already gone off
Into their next question
Before they listen to how you are
How are you?
And they're not even listening
To your answer
That's part of it
That's the human-ness dissolving
Or going away
No one's even listening to anyone anymore
It's all about processing information
The humanity is declining

The world is already ending
Someone asked me
When do I think the world is going to end
I said, not long now
Just a few more smartphones
At the dinner table
Because no one's really communicating
In the way we used to communicate
We're all now communicating
Through devices
We're together in a room
But we're all alone
Because we're all doing our own thing
Looking at our own little screens
In our own little world
Having our own little conversations
With other people
That are not in that room
Or if not actually physically doing that
Our mind is in those conversations
Or those interactions
With those other people
That are not in that room
That's what I mean by the world ending
The humanity
The humaneness of it

Is dissolving
It's going away
It's evaporating
I feel it's already ending
Who's to say there won't come a time
Where it ends completely
And it becomes something else
What will human beings evolve into
When there's no human
Or humane
Or humanity
Within anything.

THE GAME OF LIFE II

Not quite a party song
But just another song
To keep my party strong
And keep them moving on
Because it won't be long
I'm trying to build my team
And Christine
You keep on building
That field of dreams
And don't stop
Until it's done
Remember they say
If you build it
It will come
But it won't
If you don't believe, hun
So choose
We're all in a position
To set the rules
Therefore it's up to us
Whether we win or lose
Just try your best
Not to get confused
Maybe you will

Maybe you won't
Share my views
It's your move
But if I was you
And looking for a way through
I know exactly what I would do
Never surrender
There's no excuse
Might as well face the truth
You're either in it to win it
Or you're in it to lose
Now some say
Just go with the flow
But going with the flow
Could mean ending up
Somewhere you didn't want to go
So let's learn to steer the boat
To the island of our dreams
Or end up washed up
Somewhere else downstream
Far away
From where we could have been
Get my drift
Seen
Let lost hope be redeemed
And let's be extra keen

To set deadlines
And meet them
Whether they arrive on time
Or not
Let's be there to greet them
With a dedication
That can't be beaten
Whatever the weather
Because it's now or never
The goal is open now
But it won't be forever
Therefore
We must endeavour
Or remain a part
Of the minor league
Never to proceed
Never to lead
Or reach our full potential
On the scoreboard
It's a tug of war
But we can't afford
Not to score
Because to miss this
Is to miss life's final four
So with only one chance
To make it

That rarely comes twice
We better take it
Or be losers
In this game
We call life.

THE ONLY THING FOREVER IS CHANGE

I'm trying to think of a time
I've gone back
To a previous relationship
Like, got back with someone
That I've been with before
I'm trying to think of a time
I'm sure there is a time
There's definitely times
They were good ideas
For a time
To go back
And then a time came
Where it wasn't a good idea
To go back
It was a good idea at the time
But then it worked out that
It wasn't a good idea
Although
I can't take away from the fact
That at that time
The getting back was good
I can't take away from that
But then obviously
You're reminded

Why it didn't work in the first place
But then you kind of move on
There's been times
I've gone back
To previous mistakes
Previous relationships
That didn't work out
The second time around either
It's just the nature of it
I guess they kind of
Serve as reminders
Why it didn't work
The first time around
But I think it can't take away
From the fact
That when you did get back
At that moment
Or in that timeframe
It was good
Which is why you got back
But you're quickly reminded
That it was a bad idea
I wouldn't say
It's not a good idea to go back
Because people go back
And it's like

Happily ever after
And they kind of work out
What didn't go right the first time
Maybe that's the case
With the people
Who go back two or three times
And it doesn't work out
Even the fourth time
It doesn't work out
Maybe they just
Haven't worked out
Past that point where they fail
Or where it goes wrong
Maybe if they did
It would be okay
Or maybe they're just
Not meant to be together
You just don't know
It can go either way
I don't think it means
That you're not meant
To be together
I just think
It's dependent on
Different factors
It can work, or it can't work

You just find out
That you are not
Meant to be together
Or you work out what was wrong
The second time around
And you get it right
That second time around
Or later on
After being away
From the relationship
And realising
Where you both went wrong
You come back
And you come to that stage again
And you kind of know
What went wrong
And you don't go that way again
You both manage to get past it
And it's all happily ever after
Roses
Everybody happy
Or you're just not compatible
You just get to that same place
And you've done all the working out
And you've worked out
Where you went wrong

You tried to do it again
And it still doesn't work
And you think to yourself
You know what, nah
You're expecting things
To be a certain way
You think
That you know them so well
Or you think
You know them so well
That you think you know
What they're going to do
And you start assuming things
Before they even happen
And make up things in your mind
About what took place
In the way it did
And what this person is thinking
And make your own story up
In your head
About what you think they're about
And you may have it completely wrong
Which then causes friction
Which then causes ultimately
You not wanting
To be with each other

I think you're learning
About people
All the time
I think we're constantly learning
I don't think we ever
Really completely know a person
I think we're always
Going to be learning
New things about our partners
Going along
You're always going to be
Learning something new
I don't think you ever get to a point
Where you just know this person
Inside out, you know
To a degree
But I think you're always learning
Because we're always learning
About ourselves
We're always evolving ourselves
Always learning about ourselves
Our selves are always new to ourselves
All the time
So it makes sense
That we're going to be new
To someone else

All the time
And we should be
We should be evolving
We shouldn't be the same
To say that you know a person
That you can swear on your life
What they're going to do
In a certain situation
I don't think it's always the case
I don't think it's always
The right way of thinking
That you can kind of assume
Where this person is at
What they would do
When and where
And how
And then a lot of times
We end up getting it wrong
And ultimately
The relationship falls down
Or we decide
That's not the person
We thought it was
It's not going
How we thought it would go
And we don't want to be

A part of it anymore
We're always evolving
All the time
And that's why people grow
In and out of love
They either grow in
Or they grow out
Because we're always evolving
Sometimes it meets
Sometimes it doesn't
Sometimes the stars align
And sometimes they don't
But it's always moving
Change is the only thing
We can definitely guarantee
Stays the same
And will never change
The fact that change is happening
All the time
That's the one permanent thing
Change we can guarantee
Even for the human beings
That we would swear
We know them inside out
We're all evolving
As the world is.

THE TIME I STOOD HER UP

It's never been
One or the other
It's been either
I have or they have
Left the relationship
I can think of times
Where I left
And I can think of times
Where I was left
But I think
The majority fell on my side
In terms of the leaving
I remember one situation
Where I was young
A teenager
Secondary school
I was seeing a girl at the time
I was supposed to meet her
Before school
She would be at the bus stop
I would get off the bus
And meet her
I was just about to get off the bus
I was excited

Looking forward to meeting her
Over the whole weekend
The bus was driving up
To the bus stop
I'm looking out of the window
I see her
She's changed her hairstyle
I'm not feeling it
I don't like it at all
I stay on the bus
And leave her there
I don't think that was the end
Of the relationship
But it was definitely
The end of that day for us
I don't recall
If I even mentioned it
I don't know what happened after that
I clearly remember that day though
That was one situation
In that regard
But I don't think that was the end
Of the relationship
Actually, it might have been
But I don't think it was
I think I got over the hairstyle

After a while
I did not want to be seen with her
Looking like that
You know
When you're just young
And have crazy ideas
I just didn't get off the bus
I just stayed on the bus
And carried on going
I just hid myself
As the bus went by her
If I ever see her again
I'll tell her about it
But then again
I might not
Because I can't remember
If that was the last time
I saw her or not
She'd probably laugh about it now.

THE ULTIMATE GOAL

Don't forget
Every moment is something
And there's an audience
For every show
I think it's always
The right time
Reason being
Every moment is something
And there's an audience
For every show
Two things I've learned this year
We're all just making it up
As we go along
No one really knows do they
You look at your grandparents
And you realise
That they didn't even know
Or know even now
Everyone is just trying to figure it out
I think we spend our whole lives
Trying to figure out the meaning
Of why we're here
The purpose of life
The direction we're going

I think there's just more days
Where we feel comfortable
With the direction we're going in
Than other days
Some days we feel like
Oh yeah
This is it
This is what it's all about
And other days we're like
What hell was that
Everyone is still guessing
You find a level of happiness
And then you're cool with that
But you're not sure
That's the way
You should have gone
But you're happy
With the way it has turned out
The choices you made
That's a win if you're happy
But we're still guessing
It's never a negative
It's a positive
Happiness is the ultimate goal
But ultimately
We're still guessing

We're still hoping
We are making the right decisions
Along the way
No-one comes
Having it all figured out
We're all working towards
And that's what life is about
The journey is what it's most about
The experiences
The learning
The ups
The downs
It's all part of it
It's all a part of the final piece
It's exciting
It's exciting not knowing
Exciting times
I'm super excited
About what's to come.

THIS IS NOT THE END

The plantations
That were green and rich
With vegetation
Have dried up
And been left fallow
The clean clear rivers
That once ran deep
Have now become polluted
And shallow
The birds
No longer perch
And sing here
For this barren land
Would only echo
Their loneliness
The air has become toxic
And unclean
So the trees
Are unable to breathe
Too weak in their boniness
The high rocky mountains
That once harboured life
Only serve now
As tombs to harbour decease

While the seemingly
Tormented
And abandoned
Desolate land beneath them
Seems to beckon
For release
The vultures
Gather here no more
For they too would die
And wither away
In this deserted place
Of calm unrest
Nothing can live here
So nothing stays here
Nothing can graze here
So nothing ever comes here
For fear of death
For as the season changes
The cold harsh windiness
Blows its dead
Into scattered bones
And then
Into nothingness
Then comes the sun again
That once made high stench
Of rotting flesh

Now boldly returning
To claim that
Which is left
New life will come here
To this land
Again and again
And die here
Naive
To the nature of it's trend
Only few
Will live long enough
To move on
And to see
That this
Is not the end.

TO BE SOMEWHERE ELSE

I want to go
To the beach
I want to feel
The sun on my skin
And the sand
Between my toes
And the waves
Washing up my leg
I want to feel
The breeze by the sea
I want to feel care free
Careless, even
Sometimes
I couldn't care less
For all the things around me
All the things that hold me
All the things I'm committed to
Freedom
Is much more priceless
And a beautiful idea
I wish I was there
Instead of here
I wish the grind
Wasn't necessary

I wish I didn't have to
Spend time around people
Who wouldn't look twice at me
In the street
Who wouldn't even
Pour water on me
If I was on fire
It's not a great way
To spend your time
In confined spaces
Around people
Who tolerate you
Rather than celebrate you
People who gossip in corners
Unaware
That they were gossiped about too
Every time they leave the room
And laughed at
I laugh at that
It's funny to me
Anywhere, but here
Somewhere
Is where I'd rather be
I long to feel
The sun on my skin again
Walking along the beach

Without a care
To be here or there
And what a tragedy
To be where you are
Longing
To be somewhere else
What a tragedy
For peace of mind
What a tragedy for self
But nevertheless
It's something to hope for
Something to set sights on
Inside the mind
Something to motivate
Something to set designs upon
A place far away from here
A place there
Somewhere
In blue water
Under the sun.

TOMORROW

You hear that?
That's the sound
Of daylight creeping in
A new day is coming
A better day is on its way
Tomorrow is a better day
Believe that
I thought this day
Would never come
Thought we'd never see the sun
Thinking of all those
Wrongs turns I made
That turned out
To be right turns
And I'm left
Turning it over
Inside my mind
It's just a familiar place
I like to visit sometimes
Because it's crazy
When you really think about it
I don't know
What I would've done without it
The discipline

To know the difference
The discernment
To have taken
A different position
Seeing it for what it really is
And what it really isn't
Clear vision
Not blinded
By your own insistence
And limited thinking
Resistance
All the obstacles you face
That are often put in place
To completely
Slow down your pace
When you're too busy
Speeding ahead
All systems go
Thinking it's a race
When often
Exactly what you need
Is to slow down
Stop and listen
In order to know
Exactly what to do
And where to go

And what to say
Abort mission
Go this way
Go that
But that was yesterday
Today
All I can say
Is only if we knew then
What we know now
If only today knew us
Like tomorrow knows us
Just one more day
Just one more day
I see a bright morning ahead
Yes
That's what I said
Clear skies all the way
Just one more day
Brighter days are on the way
I feel so good right now
So good
It's like an awesome awakening
My head realised
The rehearsal
Is the actual thing
And my heart

Just wants to sing
I feel like a part of everything
The start
The middle
And the ending
A morning chorus to the King
For all that tomorrow brings.

TOUCH THE SUN

We slave away
For paydays
Just so we can pay
For rainy days
With the little money we've saved
Praying for a pay raise
Meanwhile
The tax man
Is preying
On what we've made
While we spend
More than we're paid
Buy more than we sell
Give more than we take
And for some
It's a living hell
And we just might break
From not coping too well
But we smoke
And drink well
And don't know
If you can tell
But we're trying
To numb the pain

Hoping things will get better
We used to run to the door
For Valentine's
And love letters
Now we run and hide
From bills
And debt collectors
We used to go out
But now we're trapped in
Behind a pile of red letters
From buying
As many things
As our bad credit would let us
And who would help us
Sooner than forget us
Like dust to dust
Good friends
Just blow away
On our bad days
Like who can we trust
But why should we fuss
When we can breathe easy
And remind ourselves
That we can be eternal
That's priceless
Why should we cuss

When all that matters
Is remembering
That what's precious
About our existence
Is internal
That's what life is
Why should we be pissed
Gold and silver
Fades away
And all the riches
In the world
Couldn't buy this
A chance to touch the sun
And uncover the god
In everyone
And though the devil's work
Is never done
I see the potential
In everyone
To let go and grow
Towards all we aim to become
To reach out and glow
As we touch the sun.

TRANSCRIBING THE FUTURE

I think about
In the future
I love the idea
Of all of the stuff
That I am recording now
In video form
Being transcribed
Into written form
Into writing
I like the idea of not knowing
What the future holds
It may be important enough
To somebody somewhere
In the future
That they actually want
To transcribe
Something I've said
And use it as a reference
I'm just in love with the idea of that
The fact that it will be there
If somebody
Should feel the need or desire
Or want to refer to it
And transcribe what's there

It's a nice thought
That it's possible
It's possible because
I've made the effort
To record it in the first place
For that to happen
That it means that much
That somebody
Would come back to it
Down the line
The things we set in motion now
Are going to have an effect
On the future
You turn left down one road
As opposed to turning right
That sets in motion
The future for everybody
Or at least
For those connected to you
Or that you come into contact with
That's amazing
Because in that sense
You are important
We have an effect on the world
Whether we like it or not
You go into a shop, for example

Your local convenience store
The shopkeeper
Behind the counter
You smile at him
Or you frown at him
It's going to have an effect
On both of you
Like how ripples work
Like energy
You can go in there and smile
And say how is your day
How are you doing
Good to see you
How's your son
Or you can go in there
And have an argument with him
It's all affective
We're affecting the world
All the time
As insignificant
As some of us think we may be
We have power
We have an effect on the world.

UNTIL THEN

I had to let you go
Maybe I'll see you
Sometime down the road
You're not the one for me
And not everybody knows
But I do
That's just the way it goes
Maybe you didn't understand
Or fully comprehend
I'm leaving this here
And moving on ahead
Please know
I meant everything I said
Perhaps organically
Somehow
Someplace
If it's meant to be
Our paths will meet again
Either way
I hope this reaches you
And if so
I leave you until then.

WHEN I'M GONE

When you go
You're remembered for a few days
People speak well of you
A few may shed a tear
Some share an endearing story or two
Maybe you'll get two weeks
If you were a popular soul
After that
Only those closest
Or who were drawn to you
Recall you on your birthdays
Then after a time
They too begin to forget
Your face
Your voice
Your words
Your energy
Eventually
We all fade from memory
And time
When I'm gone
Gather with your friends and family
And any whom share affinity for me
Set a flame to burn and release a bird

As someone reads aloud these words
Light some soft scented candles around
Lay bright and pretty flowers down
And some thoughtful words of your own
I'll be all around you and within you
Wherever you are, will be my home
When I'm gone
Choose my words carefully
Post them up on the walls
In places where men and women learn
And wherever children play
Not forgetting, where adults have fun time
And where the children study
May they all read questioningly
And thoughtfully
May they hear within, ponder and reflect
As you do now
When I'm gone
Know that I too also knew
That I could have done
And should have done much better in life
In success and achievement
In love
As a father
As a son
As a brother

As a human being
Rest assured and find some comfort
In the fact that this truth
Will never be as painful
And disappointing to bear
For you, as it always was for me
In all the places I failed you
And myself
When I'm gone
I like to think of all the women
With whom I've been closely intimate
And shared my sacred energy with
Gathered around together
With children and grandchildren
Recounting stories
And significant moments
Memories of our times together
I like to think each will say
Their encounters with me
Were uniquely special
Like no other they'd ever experienced
At any time with anyone else
And that I wasn't at fault
For not loving them
More than I loved myself
When I'm gone

I hope that my words appeal to you
Teach you and heal you
In ways I'd always aimed for in life
But knew might only be achieved
In absence
Often our words are only celebrated
Long after we've vacated
I'd made my peace with that long ago
The living ones won't proclaim to know it
Though history will plainly show it
That mainly the best poet is the dead poet
When I'm gone
Know that all wrongs towards me
Are forgiven
All transgressions forgotten
That I've taken none of them with me
They were far too heavy for the journey
And unnecessary to bear
Picture me complete
At the dawn of a new sunset
Strolling the shore
Of my souls favourite place
Smiling to the gentle crashing of waves
As the rough tide calmly rolls away
And welcomes in
A warm close of day.

WONDER OF THE SOUL

I often wonder
If the soul
Is aware of itself
Beyond this earthly shell
We call the human body
I wonder
After we die
Does our soul
Remember our names
Who we were
Where we've been
And what we've seen
And experienced in life
Or whether it just
Leaves any memory of us
Behind completely
I wonder
If it is aware of us anymore
Or just of itself
And where it is bound.

THE AUTHOR

Phoenix James is an award winning Writer, Poet, Author and Spoken Word Recording Artist. He began performing his poetic words live on stages across the UK in 1998. His debut spoken word poetry album, The A.R.T.I.S.T, was released in 2000. His first limited edition printed collection of poetry, To Whom It May Concern, was published in 2003. He has toured and performed his poetry internationally since 2004. He has appeared in films, on television and radio shows, and collaborated with other artists, singer-songwriters, actors, musicians, filmmakers and producers. In 2013, he wrote, directed and produced the feature length mock documentary film, Love Freely but Pay for Sex. Phoenix James is the author of numerous poetry books and has recorded and released several spoken word poetry albums including Phenzwaan Now & Forever, A Patchwork Remedy for A Broken Melody, FREE, Haven for the Tormented, With All That Said, Light Beams from the Void, The Love So Far, and over seventy spoken word poetry singles. All are available online now and streaming everywhere worldwide.

If you enjoyed reading this book, please leave a review or comment online. The author reads every review and they help new readers discover and experience his amazing work.

PHOENIX JAMES

Photo by Phoenix James

Phoenix James lives in London, England.

Connect with Phoenix James online via his social media platforms and let others know that you've been fortunate to discover this book. To contact or learn more about Phoenix James and his creative journey or to receive updates via his Newsletter Mailing List, visit his official website at www.PhoenixJamesOfficial.com

CHECK OUT THE AUTHOR'S OTHER
BOOK TITLES ALSO AVAILABLE
IN PAPERBACK & EBOOK

PHOENIX JAMES POETRY &
SPOKEN WORD COLLECTIONS:

LOVE, SEX, ROMANCE & OTHER BAD THINGS

ROUTE TO DESTRUCTION

DELIRIUM OF THE WISE

DON'T LET THE DAFFODILS FOOL YOU

CALL ME WHEN YOU'RE FREE

FAR FROM THE OUTSIDE

THE ONES WE DIDN'T KILL

LESSONS FROM EVERYWHERE

ANOTHER ONE FOR BURNING

A LONG BRIGHT COLD DARK SUMMER

SHAME POINT ZERO

THE SANDBAG THEORY

SOFT, SEXY & WET

BELOW BASE LEVEL

TO CATCH A PASSING UFO

NOW WE'RE TRULY BEAUTIFUL

WE ALL SHOULD BE AMAZED

DISCOVER THESE AND MUCH MORE AT
PHOENIXJAMESOFFICIAL.COM

www.ingramcontent.com/pod-product-compliance
Lightning Source LLC
Chambersburg PA
CBHW020333170426
43200CB00006B/376